KILLING WOMEN

Marisa Wegrzyn

BROADWAY PLAY PUBLISHING INC
New York
www.broadwayplaypublishing.com
info@broadwayplaypublishing.com

KILLING WOMEN
© Copyright 2014 Marisa Wegrzyn

Cover art by Stephanie Layton
First printing: January 2016
I S B N: 978-0-88145-622-6
Book design: Marie Donovan
Page make-up: Adobe Indesign
Typeface: Palatino
Printed and bound in the U S A

KILLING WOMEN was originally developed at
WordBRIDGE Playwrights Lab at Eckerd College
and the Performing Arts Department at Washington
University in Saint Louis where it was produced and
directed by William Whitaker in 2002.

KILLING WOMEN received its Chicago premiere
at Theatre Seven of Chicago. The cast and creative
contributors were:

ABBY .... Margot Bordelon
GWEN... Tracey Kaplan
LUCY ....Robin Kacyn
RAMONE ....Charlie Olson
JOE/JOHNNY/COOPER .... Brian Stojak

Director.. Brian Golden
Scenic design...John Wilson
Lighting.. Justin Wardell

CHARACTERS

ABBY, *female, 30s—wears black well*
LUCY, *female, 30s—sophisticated elegance*
GWEN, *female, 20s—a young mother*
MIKE SANDERS, *male, 30s—a co-worker*
RAMONE, *male, 50s—the boss*

played by one actor:
JOE LUNCHBOX, *male, 20s—a hit*
JOHNNY DUKE—*a hit*
COOPER—*insomniac med student*

BAXTER—GWEN's *husband (can be played by the actor playing* RAMONE *or* the actor playing JOE/JOHNNY/COOPER *depending on how fast you can make the quick change between Prologue and Scene One)*

SETTING

Various places represented simply to allow for fluid transition

ACT ONE

Prologue: Gwen's apartment
Scene 1: Lucy's apartment
Scene 2: Ramone's office
Scene 3: Gwen's apartment
Scene 4: a coffee shop
Scene 5: a back alley
Scene 6: Gwen's apartment

ACT TWO

Scene 1: Gwen's apartment
Scene 2: a bar
Scene 3: Lucy's apartment
Scene 4: a car
Scene 5: a classroom

Time: The present

ACT ONE

Prologue

(Lights on GWEN *wearing a robe, slippers.* BAXTER *and* ABBY *enter.)*

GWEN: Where have you been?

BAXTER: Working.

GWEN: Who is that?

BAXTER: Someone I work with. *(Pause)* You gonna take Tess to school today?

GWEN: What is she doing here?

ABBY: I thought you said she wasn't going to be here.

BAXTER: She wasn't going to be here.

(Pause. Triangulated awkwardness)

ABBY: Anybody wanna hear a joke?

BAXTER: Yeah.

ABBY: So this kid comes home from school. Says, "Mom, I got a problem. The boys at school are using two words I don't understand: Pussy and Bitch."
Mom says, "No big deal; pussy is like our little Mittens, and bitch is a female dog like our Sandy."
He goes to visit dad working in the garage, says "Dad, I asked mom the meaning of some words, and I don't think she told me the exact meaning."

He says, "Son, I told you, never go to your mother with these matters, she can't handle them. What are the words?"

"Pussy and bitch," says the boy.

Dad takes a *Playboy* off the shelf, circles the pubic hair of the centerfold, says, "Son, everything inside this circle is pussy."

"Okay dad, so what's 'bitch'?"

So the dad says, he says: "Everything outside that circle."

(BAXTER laughs. GWEN pulls a gun out of her robe and shoots him.)

GWEN: Would you like some coffee?

Scene One

(JOE enters with flowers, walking to LUCY's apartment. He knocks on her door. She answers.)

LUCY: Joe.

JOE: Hi, Lucy.

LUCY: What are you doing here? You look like you want to come in, would you like to come in?

(JOE enters.)

LUCY: Am I mistaken on the time? Drinks at nine o'clock?

JOE: That's right.

LUCY: It's seven o'clock. You brought flowers.

JOE: I know, I know. You said no flowers or anything. Like that. And it's only been a week, knowing you, you know? And I, well. I really like you, I really do, and I don't want to screw this up, so I thought I would, you know, make a fool of myself. With flowers. And. God, why am I so nervous? Even coming over here I had the weirdest feeling like someone was following me, you know?

LUCY: You felt like someone was following you?

JOE: Yeah, sounds stupid I know, my nerves, but—

LUCY: Were you?

JOE: Wh—

LUCY: Being followed?

JOE: I, no, I don't think so—Lucy, I just—you said we can never get into anything serious together. But. I want to plead my case to you.

LUCY: Oh, Joe.

JOE: Waddyaknow, huh? I'm falling for you.

(*Pause*)

LUCY: Can I get you something to drink?

JOE: Sure, why not? Water would be great.

(LUCY *prepares drink.*)

LUCY: Something stronger, perhaps?

JOE: Yeah, yeah, wouldn't mind something stronger. Horse tranquilizer, ha ha.

LUCY: The flowers are beautiful, Joe, really. Thank you.

JOE: Oh—I'm glad. Glad you like them. They just seemed like you, like your kind of flower. You've got a really nice apartment. Very, oh, classy. It's nice, and, uh. —I thought we could go out dancing tonight. The Red Lounge.

LUCY: The place on Broadway, yes, with the neon?

JOE: That's the place, right. With the neon.

LUCY: And the lights.

JOE: Oh, yes, the lights.

LUCY: Lovely.

(JOE *notices a tray with syringes. He picks one up.*)

JOE: Yeah, ah, they have, uh. …Live jazz.

LUCY: I've always preferred live jazz over dead jazz, any day of the week, hm. Do you know how to swing? Are you a swing kinda guy? I bet you are.

(LUCY *returns with drinks. She will casually take the syringe from* JOE *and put the tray out of the way.*)

JOE: Ah—a little. In college. Learned the basics.

LUCY: I learned the basics from that Gap ad on television. Khaki swing, do you remember that? Jump, Jive, and Wail.

JOE: Heh.

LUCY: No, I'm kidding, I learned to dance in college too, eons ago, after one of my professors invented the wheel.

JOE: You're not old, Lucy.

LUCY: I'm getting up there, Joe, be swinging a walker at The Red Lounge any day now.

JOE: Now you're just being silly, you're not old at all. Not at all. Older than me, sure, but—

(LUCY *playfully slaps* JOE's *arm.*)

JOE: —hey. You got a few good years left.

LUCY: Older than you, sure. My bones are starting to creak away the mornings.

JOE: You're beautiful. Creaky bones and all.

LUCY: Thank you.

(JOE *and* LUCY *get close. Intimate*)

JOE: Were those syringes, for, uh?

(LUCY *kisses* JOE.)

(ABBY *enters. Stands there*)

LUCY: Joe. Em. This is my…friend. Abby.

JOE: Hi. I'm Joe.

(ABBY *looks at the flowers, at* JOE, *at* LUCY.)

ABBY: *(Desi Arnaz:)* Oh, Looocy, you got some 'splaining to do.

LUCY: Finish your drink, then we'll go dancing. I promise. *(Pats his leg)*

JOE: Who is that?

LUCY: Nobody.

(ABBY *and* LUCY *aside*)

ABBY: So walk me through the chronology. I'm trying to understand what's going on here. A week ago today, Joe's scheduled to get a bullet. That obviously didn't happen.

LUCY: I had to postpone.

ABBY: If you were sick, you should've told me.

LUCY: I wasn't sick.

ABBY: I think you were, Lucy. I think you thought you had the flu, so you saw the doctor, and he said bed-rest. I have no problem telling Ramone that.

LUCY: Something worse than the flu, though.

ABBY: It's gotta be believable. Ear infection.

LUCY: Something that starts with an L.

ABBY: Leprosy is pushing it.

LUCY: Love.

ABBY: You're treading thin water with Ramone, you know that?

LUCY: I know.

ABBY: There is work and then there is everything else. You mix the two, you get your ass in a sling.

LUCY: Joe, honey, how are you doing?

JOE: *(Groggy)* I'm all, I'm all right. Almost ready to go, Luce? Luce. Lucy, I mean.

LUCY: I'll be right there, one sec.

JOE: *(To himself)* Lucy. I mean. Ready to go? *(He stumbles to the floor.)* Well that floor just came up at me.

ABBY: What's the matter with him?

LUCY: I gave him a sedative.

ABBY: Ah, no, no. None of this Florence Nightingale bullshit.

LUCY: It doesn't need to hurt any more than it has to—

JOE: Ow.

LUCY: If they would just not try to walk around.

ABBY: Do you know how much money that kid owes Ramone? He's a clown. He fucked up. You want to be Miss Nice-Nice?

LUCY: I *am* Miss Nice-Nice, boopsie.

ABBY: Well , great, that's great, I'll wait over there while you give him a complimentary blow job with his cocktail. You got your gun, you wanna blow him one, blow him a new hole.

LUCY: No more guns, not for me. The ringing in my ears keeps me up nights and, frankly, I broke a nail pulling the trigger—

ABBY: *(Overlap)* You gotta be kidding me.

LUCY: —which was the proverbial straw that broke the proverbial camel's back. If you didn't bite your nails, you'd have lovely hands. Abby, this is how I feel. Cold calculation is barbaric and doesn't suit me quite the way it suits our associates, namely, Baxter.

ABBY: Baxter is dead.

LUCY: Baxter is dead?

ABBY: Mmm hmm.

LUCY: Dead.

ABBY: *Dead.*

LUCY: What happened to him?

ABBY: Moron got shot by his wife. Ramone says I have to kill her in the morning, some payback thing.

LUCY: What are you going to do about her daughter?

ABBY: What about her daughter?

LUCY: You'd be leaving a little girl without a mother.

ABBY: That's not my problem.

(Pause)

LUCY: How was her shot?

ABBY: You shoulda seen it.

LUCY: Yeah? That good?

ABBY: Amazing.

LUCY: Amazing enough to be added to the payroll?

(Pause)

ABBY: Ramone would never hire Baxter's wife.

LUCY: Ramone hired me. Why wouldn't he hire Gwen?

ABBY: She's a mother.

LUCY: Perhaps he'll think it's a grand idea.

ABBY: He'll think it's a bonehead idea, and I'll look like the bonehead for bringing up your bonehead shit-ass idea, Lucy.

LUCY: Gwen's daughter is *adorable*. I just love children, don't you?

ABBY: Fuckin muppets.

(LUCY *goes to her hypodermics.*)

ABBY: What is that?

LUCY: Ask any anesthesiologist, putting someone to sleep is the easy part. It's waking them up that takes the Ph.D. Joe, I promise this won't hurt.

JOE: I owe you for dinner and that movie last week.

LUCY: Don't worry about it.

JOE: Yes, I do. I do. I, uh…oh, man, this is pathetic, you're gonna think I'm—I donated some blood today for the cash to pay you back. Twenty bucks. I guess they coulda taken as much blood as they wanted if I knew how this evening was gonna go. Heh…

LUCY: You donated your blood for me?

(JOE *nods*)

LUCY: That's the most romantic thing anyone has ever done for me.

ABBY: Lucy. Don't do this again. Don't date, don't fall in love, don't get involved with anybody you have to kill.

(LUCY *gets* JOE *to his feet. They dance.* ABBY *watches.*)

LUCY: Promised you a dance, didn't I?

JOE: You're beautiful. Good dancer. Nicer if we had some music. Some jazz, slow jazz, with a heavy bass, something beautiful. So beautiful.

(LUCY *searches out a vein in his neck as they dance. She slides the needle into a vein. Sensual for both.* ABBY *exits. Lights*)

Scene Two

(RAMONE's *office.* ABBY *and* RAMONE)

RAMONE: Gwen Goralski? Baxter's wife?

ABBY: The girl can kill.

RAMONE: Baxter's wife?

ABBY: She was impressive, she was clean, and she didn't even do it for a paycheck. Yet.

(RAMONE *pours a bottle of Mylanta into a glass and adds whiskey.*)

RAMONE: I'm going to have to say no.

ABBY: Why?

RAMONE: She has a kid.

ABBY: You hired Baxter when you knew he had a daughter.

RAMONE: That's different.

ABBY: How is that different?

RAMONE: It's different 'cause it's different. You can be a real pest sometime. Say I hold grudges, Baxter was one of my best.

ABBY: Why no?

(*Pause*)

RAMONE: I'm an asshole now, is that it?

ABBY: I could drive a truck through your asshole.

RAMONE: Don't think I haven't been listening to you, 'cause I have, and that's why I say no, and don't call me an insensitive prick. I hired you in the first place, didn't I?

ABBY: And I was so glad to be your calling card novelty. And then you went and hired goddamn Baxter to take my place.

RAMONE: I hired Baxter when business went boom.

ABBY: You gave him the heavy hitters, Ramone. The guy's a fuck-wad to me, and I was left with the scooby doo crowd, blowing their allowance on weekend little league.

RAMONE: I was trying to alleviate your complaints. *(Clutches his stomach)*

ABBY: I don't remember complaining I was earning too much money. *(Referring to his stomach pain:)* What's the matter?

RAMONE: Stomach.

ABBY: Why are you giving me shit jobs?

RAMONE: You said nobody was taking you seriously, so I was giving you the ones—would you listen—I was giving you the ones that were least likely to give you a hard time.

ABBY: *(*Overlap above)* You're giving me shit.

RAMONE: *(His stomach again:)* Ugh... I am being considerate of your thoughts and feelings.

ABBY: Oh, and Baxter just happened to be stuck with the corporate lawyers, C E Os...

RAMONE: I can't change the goddamn world, can I?

ABBY: ...Hand surgeons? There's like two really good ones in the country and he gets to kill both of them?

RAMONE: I got an ulcer 'cause a you, Abby.

ABBY: What about Gwen?

RAMONE: What about her?

ABBY: We bring her in.

RAMONE: I already told you no.

ABBY: You owe me. Do I ever brownnose like Miles? Or drive a car through the window of a Kinko's like Mike Sanders?

RAMONE: You left Wyatt off your list.

(Pause)

ABBY: You look like hell, Ramone.

RAMONE: That good, huh?

ABBY: Maybe it's your lifestyle. Maybe you should take up tennis. You'd look great in shorts.

(MIKE enters.)

RAMONE: What happened to the car?

MIKE: Car's a little broken.

RAMONE: What happened?

MIKE: I messed up Kinko's. Hi, Abby.

ABBY: Mike Sanders.

RAMONE: Is the car functional?

MIKE: Oh. I meant to tell you. I sorta crashed Wyatt's car.

RAMONE: Where'd your car go?

MIKE: I lost my car keys.

RAMONE: Wyatt's gotta work tonight and he has no car, you realize that, Mike?

MIKE: Sorry, Ramone.

RAMONE: He's gotta have a car. Abby, gimmie your car keys.

ABBY: Excuse me?

RAMONE: Give me your car keys.

ABBY: I'm not giving my car to Wyatt.

RAMONE: Is that your car, Abby? Did you pay for that fine automobile with the leather interior?

MIKE: And cup holders.

RAMONE: They go to who I say they go, and I say that Wyatt gets your car tonight. Mike's car is outta commission, Wyatt's car is outta commission, be generous enough to let Wyatt use your car tonight.

ABBY: My spare gun is in the glove compartment. And what about my C D in the player?

MIKE: Which C D you listening to?

ABBY: An album called "I'm Going to Break Your Face If You Don't Find Your Car Keys."

(ABBY *hands her keys to* RAMONE.)

RAMONE: Thank you, Abby. Mike, we'll talk about this later, I gotta talk with Abby. Why don't you go on home?

MIKE: Yeah. Yeah, okay. Bye, Abby. (*He exits.*)

ABBY: Does he sniff glue?

RAMONE: Look Abby, I'm gettin' some surgery in a couple weeks. Someone's covering the week I'm outta commission.

ABBY: Who?

RAMONE: I'm stepping aside for more than that week. Probably for good. I'll still be around, still part of the racket, but I'm leaving the big stress for someone else.

ABBY: Who's taking your place?

RAMONE: Wyatt.

ABBY: You know I've been with you longer than Wyatt's been with you.

RAMONE: Yeah.

ABBY: Doesn't that mean anything?

RAMONE: Yeah, Abbs, it means a lot.

(*Pause*)

ABBY: This is bullshit.

RAMONE: Don't get me wrong. You got a fantastic shot.

ABBY: I deserve the promotion.

RAMONE: You got the details, you take care a business.

ABBY: What does Wyatt have that I don't?

RAMONE: Abby, I'm asking you to kill Gwen and you're fighting me on it.

ABBY: Because I think she'd do a good job.

RAMONE: Can you kill a woman?

ABBY: What kind of a question is that?

RAMONE: Can you kill a woman?

ABBY: Of course I can kill a woman.

RAMONE: What about Lucy?

ABBY: She's working out isn't she? I told you she'd take to this.

RAMONE: When you had to kill Lucy, you convinced me to hire her, she turned out to be a real bed of roses, didn't she? Miles mentioned she's not using her gun anymore, is this true?

ABBY: I'll make her go back to the gun.

RAMONE: She's been nothing but a pain in my ass since day one.

ABBY: Ramone, I'm working with her to get it right.

RAMONE: Abby, can you kill a woman?

ABBY: Yes.

RAMONE: Kill Gwen.

ABBY: You saw what she did to Baxter. A shot like that isn't beginner's luck. You can't tell me you haven't at least considered bringing Gwen in.

RAMONE: It was a clean shot. But she shot *Baxter*. Gwen shot Baxter. There are consequences.

ABBY: Gwen shot Baxter, that's why you should hire her.

RAMONE: She's a mother. She's got a kid. What's she gonna do, a drive-by on the way to Chuck E Cheese.

ABBY: You give me one week with Gwen, I will train her to do this job.

RAMONE: You think you can train *her* in a week?

ABBY: Yeah.

RAMONE: Do you have any idea what you would be getting yourself into?

ABBY: Firing a gun is simple stuff.

RAMONE: I'm not talking about that half of it.

ABBY: Then what are you talking about?

RAMONE: You got one week to train Gwen.

ABBY: All right.

RAMONE: If she doesn't take to it in a week, you have to kill Gwen. And her daughter.

ABBY: No problem.

RAMONE: Is it really?

ABBY: No problem.

RAMONE: I'll check in next Sunday.

ABBY: That's not a week. Today's Monday, I should get till next Monday.

RAMONE: Monday, Tuesday, Wednesday, Thursday, Friday, Saturday, Sunday. That's seven days, that's a week. Scrounging for every minute you can get. Aren't you even going to ask how you'll know if she's ready for this job?

ABBY: I think I'll know when she's ready.

RAMONE: And I will make sure you know when that is. *(He takes a swig of his Mylanta and whiskey.)*

ABBY: I hope that shit rips your stomach a new hole.

Scene Three

(GWEN's apartment. ABBY slams a heavy gun into GWEN's palm.)

GWEN: Uhh.

ABBY: You've used one before.

GWEN: Yeah, but—

ABBY: —Aim, pull the trigger. How old are you?

GWEN: I'm, I'm, Twenty-five?

ABBY: Are you asking me if you're twenty five?

GWEN: No no I'm twenty-five. Twenty six next,—

ABBY: *(Interrupt)* You look twelve.

GWEN: —next month.

ABBY: *(Hands paper and photograph GWEN)* Johnny Duke, one-ten South Main. That's where he lives. That's his face, don't forget it.

GWEN: I'm sorry, who is this?

ABBY: Johnny Duke. You're going to kill him.

GWEN: Um, noooooo. No. I'm not, uh, my husband, that was his work, I'm not, uh. A *murderer*.

ABBY: You did kill your husband, right?

GWEN: W—well.

ABBY: You shot Baxter point blank.

GWEN: Well. Y—sorta.

ABBY: You'll do just fine. I'll be with you the first time, all right. Me and you. Tomorrow morning. He's got a routine, we'll follow him, he goes to this coffee place—

GWEN: Tomorrow morning?

ABBY: Yeah.

GWEN: I have to take Tess to school in the morning.

ABBY: Tess.

GWEN: My daughter.

ABBY: Can't she just hitchhike?

GWEN: She's *five*. What if I said I don't want to do this job?

ABBY: What if I said you had no choice?

GWEN: You can go tell Ramone I put my foot down on this whole arrangement. Please leave.

ABBY: Leave?

GWEN: Leave.

ABBY: You should at least think about this.

GWEN: I have thought about this.

ABBY: It seems hasty.

GWEN: I'm—I'm. Well, I'm done and that's that.

ABBY: You're leaving me with a lot of paper work. We need to talk compensation, nullified contracts, carbon copies, and oh lordy, I gotta run through personnel, find a temp--all these channels of bureaucracy, you know.

GWEN: Abby—

ABBY: —In the meantime, we'll just have to divvy your work to Miles, Mike Sanders, Wyatt, Lucy. All this extra work you're giving me. It's like a homework assignment from a substitute teacher--I just don't wanna do it. So I'll kill your daughter instead.

GWEN: You can't be serious.

(ABBY *pulls out gun.*)

No, Abby! Not Tess!

ABBY: Did you think I wasn't serious?

GWEN: You can't do this to me!

ABBY: I'm not the one doing it. Ramone has his claws in both of us, I can only do so much for you.

(ABBY *grabs a teddy bear from the floor. Holds a gun to its head. A long silence. They look offstage towards Tess's bedroom. ABBY hides gun and teddy bear behind her back. Tess should be an offstage presence*)

GWEN: Tess, honey, go back to bed.

ABBY: Maybe she wants water.

GWEN: I think I know my own daughter! *(Beat)* Do you want some water? Tess, will you ask instead of just nodding? I'll get you some water, okay? *(Looks at Tess through hands like binoculars)* I seeeeeee yooooou, squeaky bear. You're not in bed, are you? Ya can't hide from me.

ABBY: What are you doing?

GWEN: It's just something we do.

ABBY: Why?

GWEN: Because we like it.

ABBY: Why?

GWEN: It's something special between the two of us.

ABBY: Why won't she come over here?

GWEN: She's shy. Tess, hop into bed, I'll be there in a minute, okay?

ABBY: All right—it's getting late—I'll be here tomorrow morning, six A M.

GWEN: I can't just leave Tess by herself.

ABBY: Why not?

GWEN: Abby, she is five years old! She needs help getting ready for school in the morning and she needs to be dropped off, I can't take off looking for this *guy* just because you say so. I can't do this.

ABBY: Yes you can.

GWEN: I have a child, don't you understand what that means?

ABBY: Yeah, it means I have to get you fucking babysitter!

(ABBY *goes to the phone, considers who to call. Then dials. Lights up on* MIKE)

MIKE: Hulloo.

ABBY: Mike, it's Abby, what are you doing tomorrow morning?

(*Mike is smiling into the phone*)

Hello?

MIKE: Hi, Abby.

ABBY: Are you busy tomorrow?

MIKE: Uh, when'd you say tomorrow?

ABBY: Morning. I need a babysitter.

MIKE: A babysitter? You got a baby?

ABBY: N—no. There's this kid.

MIKE: Tomorrow morning, lemmie see… Ohhh, shoot! Shoot, Abby, shoot. I got a hit tomorrow, like—wait, like when in the morning?

ABBY: Six a.m., can you do six?

MIKE: Ohhhh shoot. No, I can't, Abby. Dangit! I can't.

ABBY: All right.

MIKE: I really would like to babysit, might be good fun, but I gotta cap that bowling alley guy by six thirty in the ol' a.m., and shoot, Abby, I'm really sorry I can't help you out.

ABBY: That's all right.

MIKE: Shoot.

ABBY: It's all right, Mike. I gotta go.

MIKE: I'm writing haiku poetry right now.

ABBY: You're what?

MIKE: Do you want to hear one? A Haiku poem. It's Japanese.

ABBY: You know Japanese?

MIKE: It's a form of poetry that's supposed to capture the essence of something specific, like a raindrop on a rock or perhaps the green of a turtle. You wanna hear one?

ABBY: Uh…

MIKE: It's short. This one's called "Laundry": (*He counts the syllables on his fingers as he recites.*)
Pile of dirty clothes
Shirts on the bottom will be
Cleaned by compression
…I've never shared my poetry with anybody before. You're the first.

ABBY: Mike. I gotta go.

(*Lights go down on* MIKE.)

(ABBY *dials a phone number.*)

(*Lights up on* LUCY)

LUCY: This is Lucy.

ABBY: I need a favor.

LUCY: A favor, ohhh, Abby needs a favor.

ABBY: Are you busy tomorrow morning?

(GWEN *will raise her gun, unnoticed by* ABBY.)

LUCY: Why?

ABBY: I need you to baby-sit.

LUCY: A child?

ABBY: No, a llama—of course a child. Gwen's daughter.

LUCY: She's adorable, isn't she?

ABBY: Eh.

LUCY: I'm glad Gwen's daughter doesn't look anything
like Baxter; I always thought he looked like one of
those rare, wrinkly dogs inbred for their weirdness. I'm
not suggesting that a relationship should be founded
on aesthetics.

ABBY: What the fuck are you talking ab—can you baby-
sit or what?

LUCY: I'm awfully busy busy busy. When do you need
me to baby-sit?

(GWEN *puts the gun to* ABBY's *head, clicks off the safety.*
GWEN *is stone-cold scary in kill mode:)*

GWEN: He wouldn't listen to me either. What I said
never mattered, ever, not ever, not at all. If I wanted
him to listen, I'd have to make him listen. If this is the
language he understood, then it's the language I would
speak. The night before, I took all of Tess's pictures and
art off the refrigerator so they wouldn't get sprayed
with blood. He heard me loud and clear. *(Pause)* My
daughter shouldn't see me like this.

LUCY: Let me talk to Gwen.

ABBY: Lucy wants to talk to you.

GWEN: Who's Lucy?

ABBY: The baby-sitter.

(GWEN *takes the phone. Keeps gun on* ABBY)

LUCY: Hi Gwen, this is Lucy. How are you doing?

GWEN: I'm…fine?

LUCY: Well, you lower that gun when you're good and ready to lower that gun. It gets heavy, believe me, and I personally hate using one myself. I broke a nail last week, it was, ugh, it was depressing. Isn't that just so girly? So, I was thinking, I have a coupon for a two for one manicure at Happy Nails, they're wonderful. Heaven. *Heaven.* I'm looking for someone to join me when I go on Friday and Abby certainly won't go—she bites her nails, nasty habit. So, Friday, how about it, Gwen?

GWEN: Friday. Sure. Sure. Okay.

LUCY: Oh, lovely. That's lovely. Did you know I live in the building right across the street from you? Go to your window. Third floor. See?

(LUCY *waves.* GWEN *waves back.*)

GWEN: I've seen you before.

LUCY: In the neighborhood.

GWEN: Yes.

LUCY: What time do you need me to baby sit tomorrow?

GWEN: Um.

LUCY: Why don't you ask Abby.

GWEN: What time should Lucy come over?

ABBY: Six.

GWEN: Six.

LUCY: I'll see you bright and early at six.

GWEN: What are your qualifications?

LUCY: My qualifications?

GWEN: With children. Do you have references?

LUCY: References. No. I'm sorry, I don't, Gwen. Do you need references?

GWEN: Do you have any experience with children?

LUCY: Ah, well, I understand them as a concept and I think they're a great idea!

(GWEN *stares at the phone.*)

LUCY: Hello? Gwen?

(GWEN *hands the phone to* ABBY. GWEN *exits.*)

ABBY: What did you say to her?

LUCY: Where did she go?

ABBY: What did you *say*?

LUCY: I've never baby sat before. I said I don't have any baby sitting references.

ABBY: Oh, like she was really gonna check. I'll tell her you're Mary Fucking Poppins.

LUCY: Abby.

ABBY: What?

LUCY: Spoonful of sugar with this one, hm?

(LUCY *hangs up, lights down on her.* ABBY *stands with the phone listening to the sound of* GWEN *puking off stage.* ABBY *will light up a cigarette and smoke.*)

ABBY: Hey. So I was watching these guys race in this marathon last week. Every other person who stumbled over the finish line had something in their gut to puke up, and I'm like, what the fuck? People do this to themselves? They run until they gak all over the street in front of hundreds of people throwing fuckin Dixie Cups of water at em? Stupid. So I figure, maybe, after I thought about it, there's gotta be something that makes the puking worth it. They're worthwhile things, marathons, cause you finish and you feel like a million bucks even when you cough up your cookies. 'Course I wasn't near all the puke. But I saw it through my scope; I could tell they all felt like a million bucks. Except for the guy I shot.

GWEN: *(Offstage)* Are you smoking?

ABBY: Maybe.

GWEN: *(Offstage)* Please don't smoke.

ABBY: The window's open.

GWEN: *(Offstage)* I don't want Tess to think that smoking is cool.

ABBY: Smoking is cool.

(GWEN enters. ABBY will extinguish her cigarette and take out a tin of Altoids. She will offer one to GWEN who will take one.)

ABBY: What did you and Lucy talk about?

GWEN: We're going to get a manicure. She has a coupon. Two for one.

ABBY: Really.

GWEN: Friday.

ABBY: She didn't ask me to get a manicure.

GWEN: Lucy says you bite your nails.

ABBY: Well I wouldn't bite my nails if I knew I was getting a free fucking manicure. *(Offers Altoids)*

GWEN: I don't have the stomach for this job.

ABBY: And while you may not have the stomach for this job, you sure got the poise for it. That's the truth. I nearly pissed myself when you clicked the safety. That was good. Forget how scary that shit is sometimes.

GWEN: This is all very upsetting.

ABBY: Gwen…

GWEN: Yes?

ABBY: We gotta talk about your clothes.

GWEN: My clothes?

ABBY: That Land's End number you got on is ka ka.

GWEN: Is that how you always dress?

ABBY: You know what they say about black. Might do wonders for you.

GWEN: Did you just call me fat?

ABBY: …No.

GWEN: I'm not stupid, I read *Cosmo*.

ABBY: All I'm saying is you would look great in black.

GWEN: It's not like it's your clothes that kill people.

ABBY: Oh, Gwen, your clothes are killing me right now. *(Takes off her coat)* Put this on.

GWEN: Why?

ABBY: Put it on.

GWEN: I don't want to wear your coat, it's warm in here.

ABBY: Put on the coat.

GWEN: I don't want to p—

ABBY: Put on the coat. You'll *like* it.

(GWEN puts on the coat.)

ABBY: Damn, Gwen. If looks could kill, you'd be queen of the slaughterhouse. Hey, look, what I said before. I wasn't really gonna do anything to your kid, okay? That Teddy Bear, I dunno, could be fucked. But I wasn't, you know, I wasn't gonna, you know. You know?

(GWEN *gives back the coat*)

GWEN: Goodnight, Abby. *(She exits.)*

(ABBY *lights a cigarette, picks up the Teddy Bear. Looks at it. Blows smoke in its face. Lights.)*

Scene Four

(A coffee shop. ABBY, *still smoking, sits at one table with a coffee cup.* GWEN *sits nearby, but not with* ABBY. GWEN *has a copy of* Cosmo, *but is trying to keep her eye on* JOHNNY DUKE *who sits out of earshot from* ABBY *and* GWEN.*)*

GWEN: You didn't tell me we'd have to sit in a coffee place with smoking. I have terrible circulation and cigarette smoke constricts the blood vessels leading to even worse circulation. And I read in *Newsweek*, like, seventy percent of all open heart surgeries are due to smoking-related illness. F Y I.

ABBY: Stop talking to me.

GWEN: Who else am I supposed to talk to?

ABBY: Keep your eye on him.

GWEN: And then what?

ABBY: If he leaves, you follow him.

GWEN: And then what?

ABBY: You wait until nobody's around.

GWEN: And then what?

ABBY: You're gonna "and then what" me into a coma, Gwen; you *know what*.

GWEN: Do you have a pen?

ABBY: Why?

GWEN: I want to do the quiz in here: twenty questions to find out if I play hard-to-get.

ABBY: If you are doing a quiz you are not paying attention, are you?

GWEN: No?

ABBY: Correct.

GWEN: Can I ask you a question?

ABBY: Is it about work?

GWEN: Sort of, but not really.

ABBY: Then no.

GWEN: All right. Guess what?

ABBY: *What*?

GWEN: *(Producing pen from her bag)* Chicken butt.

(ABBY gets up and takes the magazine and pen away from GWEN, goes back to her table.)

GWEN: I feel like I should call Lucy, make sure everything went all right getting Tess to school this morning. I'm sure everything was fine, but I've never left Tess with a baby sitter before. I'm sure she's fine. I'm sure. And everything's fine and I'm worrying for no good reason. I do that, I worry, I've always been like that but it's always nice to have somebody to talk to about it, to settle my nerves.

ABBY: You make me wish I was autistic.

GWEN: *(Standing)* I have to go to the restroom. Or is that *not allowed*?

(GWEN exits. ABBY keeps her eye on JOHNNY, but peeks into the magazine between surveillance.)

(LUCY, with coffee, and GWEN enter.)

LUCY: …and the hierarchy that goes on, my goodness. All those cars jockeying for position, a battle of "who can get closest to the main entrance to deposit their offspring" It is really fascinating. I felt like Margaret Mead. Then there's that *bus lane*.

GWEN: I should've told you about that bus lane.

LUCY: Wellll, I exchanged a few words with that crossing guard, but he was unmerciful. Unmerciful. Not as unmerciful, though, as the woman in that green Jeep Cherokee.

ABBY: What are you doing here?

LUCY: Tess is wonderful. Such a charming little girl.

GWEN: She's pretty wonderful.

LUCY: Anytime you need a babysitter.

GWEN: You two got on all right.

LUCY: Fabulously.

ABBY: Lucy.

GWEN: She didn't need me or anything?

LUCY: Oh, no, not at all, she was showing *me* what to do.

GWEN: Oh. That's good.

LUCY: With her cereal and the milk and the raisins.

GWEN: I usually do that for her. She is particular about it.

ABBY: Lucy.

LUCY: Excuse me. What?

(*Aside with* LUCY)

ABBY: Gwen is working.

LUCY: (*Noticing* JOHNNY) Are you insane?

ABBY: If she can get Johnny Duke, she can get anyone.

LUCY: Wyatt couldn't even get Johnny Duke.

ABBY: Wyatt is a dumbass.

LUCY: She is going to get hurt.

ABBY: She'll be fine.

LUCY: This is a terrible idea.

ABBY: I only have few more days to get her into shape.

LUCY: A few days is not enough time to train anybody to do this job.

ABBY: If she gets Johnny Duke, she will impress the hell out of Ramone. She needs to impress Ramone. You understand?

(Beat)

LUCY: Johnny Duke. My goodness. If he weren't such an asshole he'd almost be my type.

ABBY: How come you didn't tell me about your free manicure? I coulda gone.

LUCY: You bite your nails.

ABBY: So?

LUCY: Generally a manicurist needs something to manicure.

(JOHNNY approaches GWEN.)

LUCY: Oh my God.

ABBY: Wait.

LUCY: Abby.

ABBY: Let her deal.

JOHNNY: Couldn't help noticing you glancing my way. So where we going to dinner tonight?

GWEN: Dinner?

JOHNNY: Mmm. Friendly invitation.

GWEN: Oh. Ha ha. 'Cause I thought it was a pick up line. Ha ha. *(Desperate glance to ABBY and LUCY)*

JOHNNY: You wanna invite your girlfriends over. Make it a foursome.

GWEN: Oh, ha ha, yeah. Yeah. *(Waves* ABBY *and* LUCY *over)*

ABBY: Shit.

*(*ABBY *and* LUCY *join* GWEN *and* JOHNNY.*)*

JOHNNY: Howdy. Name's Johnny Duke.

ABBY: That's quite a name.

JOHNNY: Is it?

ABBY: Sounds like you chop wood for fun.

*(*JOHNNY *stands.)*

JOHNNY: If you'll excuse me, ladies. Gonna get me a refill. You sit tight. I'll be back in a flash. *(He exits.)*

LUCY: Well that was lovely, Abby, now he knows something's up.

GWEN: You said he didn't know who we are.

ABBY: He doesn't.

LUCY: We're faceless beauties in this world, Gwen.

GWEN: But he was hitting on me.

LUCY: It's part of our appeal in the business unless, of course, you let on that you're more than your parts. Then, of course, you become less affective.

ABBY: Oh?

LUCY: In general, yes. You see, Gwen, our *reason d'etre* is to first and foremost be unsuspected as a threat. Johnny Duke, who has gone to refresh his latte thinks...now why was that bitch uppity with me?

ABBY: So I'm an ineffective bitch.

LUCY: Abby. Please.

ABBY: You, Lucy, of all people, are calling me inaffective.

LUCY: I think you could have gotten Gordy Laroux last week.

ABBY: Nobody has been able to get Gordy Laroux

LUCY: Nobody, net yet, because you "copped a 'tude" and sent up red flags.

ABBY: I didn't "cop a 'tude." And who says "cop a 'tude", Lucy, don't ever say that again.

LUCY: The phrase was implied in quotations—and *maybe*...just maybe, now, you understand...maybe he became suspicious when you said you were going to cut off his dick and use it as a Whack-A-Mole mallet.

GWEN: That's really gross.

LUCY: Had you been me in that situation, Gordy Laroux would be no more, simply, a handful of dust and la la la.

ABBY: Had I been *you*? His dick would've been in my mouth after dinner and a movie. *(To* GWEN*)* Don't *date* the prey. It's *inaffective*.

LUCY: Then Abby, if you're so affective, how come the promotion is going to Wyatt? Hm?

GWEN: Who's Wyatt?

LUCY: A co-worker.

ABBY: Look—I work my ass off. I am working my ass off right now.

GWEN: I don't think sitting here drinking coffee with me is a lot of work.

ABBY: You have *no idea*. I'm not setting off any fire alarms, but if you haven't noticed, we have the rough spot in this business.

LUCY: So you didn't get promoted because you're not a man and you're ineffective because you're not much of a woman.

(Pause)

ABBY: I don't see you getting promoted.

LUCY: I don't want a promotion.

ABBY: You'd foam at the mouth for it.

LUCY: I would foam at the nothing for it. Ramone's job? I'll pass on having an ulcer before age forty, thankyouverymuch. And stress causes premature aging and wrinkles.

GWEN: That is so true.

ABBY: I deserve the promotion.

GWEN: According to *Cosmo,* stress is almost as bad as smoking. There is also a great article in here about fashionable footwear for the gal on the go, and another article on anger and how it takes years off your life.

(ABBY grabs the magazine and whips it across the coffee shop.)

LUCY: Of the three of us: me, you, or Gwen—oh, here's the Pepsi Challenge—who, truly, is the most affective executioner. I think it's Gwen.

ABBY: *Gwen.*

LUCY: Because she—unlike, obviously, me or you—Gwen is a mother, therefore, she is an unrecognized asset to a society that employs executioners.

GWEN: An asset.

LUCY: What is execution but, literally, the opposite of who we are? The nature of nurture. Bearer of life. Who better to take life than the one who endured the labor. Our job is not mindless, indifferent violence, nor is it senseless murder, it is a *job*. It is work. But there is compassion. There is. Right Abby? There are some jobs better suited for women; killing happens to be one of them. You'll find that in the end, with a last breath, they all want their mommies.

(JOHNNY *enters with a refill and another drink he sets in front of* GWEN.)

JOHNNY: Thought you could use a warm up.

GWEN: Um. Thanks.

JOHNNY: *(To* ABBY *and* LUCY*)* I only have two hands. You understand.

ABBY: Gwen, since you and Johnny seem to be sweet on each other, why don't you take him out back in the alley, give him a little something-something.

GWEN: Can I go home?

ABBY: Gwen. Now would be a good time to take care of our new friend Johnny Duke.

GWEN: Well, um. Johnny. Do you want a little…um… something-something. In the alley?

JOHNNY: I wouldn't say no to a little something-something from a sweetheart like you.

GWEN: How about we meet up in the back in a few. Okay?

JOHNNY: Can't wait. *(He exits.)*

GWEN: Aren't you going to come with me?

LUCY: I know it's your first time and maybe you're a little scared but this is going to be a magical moment for you and you never forget your first. Oh, Abby, can I watch?

ABBY: She's gotta learn to do it on her own.

LUCY: Like a little bird punted from the nest must learn to fly.

ABBY: Gwen, I know you just wanna pop that motherfucker between the eyes, right?

GWEN: Well—

ABBY: Right?!

GWEN: I don't know! Yes?

ABBY: Yes!

GWEN: Yes!

LUCY: This is so exciting. Gwen—I'm excited for you.

GWEN: Okay! Let's do it! *(She runs out. She re-enters for her purse.)* I forgot my gun. *(She exits.)*

(Pause)

LUCY: She's been out there a long time.

ABBY: She's been out there five seconds.

(Pause. ABBY begins biting her nails)

LUCY: You really shouldn't do that.

ABBY: I like to rip my nails off with my teeth. It's soothing.

LUCY: Manicures are soothing too.

(Pause. ABBY and LUCY check their watches. GWEN enters.)

GWEN: Okay, I have to go pick Tess up from school now. It's only a half-day program.

ABBY: Did you…

GWEN: Oh, yeah—It went fine—but I just realized I'm going to be late to pick her up, so I have to go.

ABBY: Wait—you—you did it?

GWEN: Yeah. Um. Well…what do I do with… *(Mouths: "the body")*

ABBY: What?

GWEN: The—his—you know—his body. Do I just leave him there?

ABBY: No you don't just leave him there. You find a fuckin dumpster.

GWEN: I have to touch him?

ABBY: Yes.

GWEN: Do I *have* to? Instead of touching him, could I just *not* touch him?

LUCY: Gwen, it's not as bad as it seems. You'll get used to it after the first few times. The first few times, yes, those are the awful times. It's *awful*. Oh my good lord, it's awful. But after you get over it, then it's all right. It's not great. You're never going to wake up in the morning and say "I can't wait to drag so and so down five flights of stairs." Well, this one time I did wake up saying that, but it was special circumstances.

GWEN: I don't want to get blood on my clothes.

LUCY: I *hate* getting blood on my clothes. We have so much in common. You know, Gwen, there are… alternative methods in this industry. This is not the Wild West and the gun is not the law of the land.

ABBY: You are not teaching her the shit with the needles.

GWEN: What—with the needles?

LUCY: She wants to know.

ABBY: She has a body to deal with.

LUCY: She wants to *know*. She wants to *learn*.

ABBY: Where—Lucy—where are you going?

LUCY: I am going to compose a syllabus in a twelve point Helvetica font. Gwen: you are going to *love* it. (*She exits.*)

GWEN: Abby, I really have to go pick up Tess.

ABBY: You're gonna pick up that body before you pick up your kid. Every job has its shit, and you learn to fucking cope or you don't get the paycheck. When I was a flight attendant, do you know how much bullshit I had to deal with?

GWEN: You were a flight attendant?

ABBY: Yeah.

GWEN: Really?

ABBY: You don't think I could be a flight attendant? Hey, if you think killing people is tough, try saying "thank you" when someone hands you their garbage. Thank you for giving me your shit, let me go frame it. I made the job work for me. You can't smoke on the airplane, right? So I'd go into the bathroom, light a cigarette, take a deep drag and exhale into the toilet right as I flushed it. Those vacuum toilets are phenomenal, but you only get one drag and one flush before the fucking smoke detector goes off. The moral of the story is suck it up and get rid of Johnny.

GWEN: Will you do it this time and I promise to learn how to do it next time?

ABBY: I'm not cleaning up your shit.

GWEN: Will you please do it? Just this once?

ABBY: Do I look like your maid? Do you have a maid, and do I look like her. Because you seem confused.

GWEN: I really wouldn't ask if I wasn't in a hurry, but I need to go pick up my daughter. Please.

(Pause)

ABBY: Now this is the one and only time.

GWEN: Absolutely.

ABBY: As long as that's clear.

GWEN: Crystal. Oh, thank you, Abby. Thank you. You know, I would be interested in learning the way Lucy does it. Maybe this won't be a problem for me if there isn't as much, you know, potential for splatter. Anyway, really, thank you.

ABBY: Would you just go already?

(GWEN *exits.*)

ABBY: I don't get paid nearly enough.

Scene Five

(ABBY *enters. She is dragging* JOHNNY's *body.* MIKE *enters.*)

MIKE: Hi, Abby.

ABBY: Mike Sanders.

MIKE: What're you doin'?

ABBY: Dragging a body.

MIKE: You wanna get some ice cream?

ABBY: What are you doing here?

MIKE: Supposed to meet Wyatt 'round here. We were gonna go to Hot Knockers.

ABBY: Hot Knockers in the middle of the day?

MIKE: There's a forty cent buffalo wing lunch special from eleven to three, in addition to pole dancing, which I appreciate for the athleticism. Wyatt had to postpone Hot Knockers for a last-minute meeting with Ramone, so I had some unexpected time to enjoy the day. Walked by the coffee shop, saw you through the window. Oh! Wyatt thanked me for crashing his car because he likes your car, everything except for the radio stations programmed into the buttons.

ABBY: Now that pisses me off. You don't fuck with the presets.

MIKE: I'm real sorry you had to give up your keys. Can I make it up to you?

ABBY: I love my car.

MIKE: You look real good driving that car.

ABBY: I look awesome.

MIKE: What's that car's color? Cinnamon Bronze?

ABBY: Autumn sunburst.

MIKE: Hey, can I make it up to you some other way? Like I could buy you ice cream.

ABBY: Can't you see I'm busy?

MIKE: I'm talking ice cream after. There's a really great ice cream place just opened up they have a cappuccino cookie dough blast that's amazing. And you can get any mix-in smashed into your ice cream. *(Looking at* JOHNNY*)* Wow! Nice shot! Nice. That's real marksmanship, Abby. I'd even go as far to say you got the best shot of any of us now.

ABBY: It's, uh…it's not my shot.

MIKE: It's not.

ABBY: No.

MIKE: Who did that?

ABBY: Gwen.

MIKE: Who's Gwen?

ABBY: Gwen Goralski.

MIKE: Baxter's *wife*? Holy cow. What a shot. Where's Gwen, she's not here?

ABBY: She had to go.

MIKE: It's nice of you to clean up her stuff.

ABBY: Some would say I'm too nice.

MIKE: I wouldn't say that.

ABBY: *(Drags body)* They don't always look heavy, sometimes they're just dense.

MIKE: I'm probably dense too.

ABBY: Yeah, but I don't have to drag you around.

MIKE: I don't think you could.

ABBY: You don't think I could?

MIKE: Nope.

ABBY: I could drag you down the goddamn street.

MIKE: No you couldn't.

ABBY: Get on the ground.

MIKE: You want me to get on the ground?

ABBY: Get on the ground, Mike.

(MIKE does. ABBY drags him by the feet.)

MIKE: This is fun.

ABBY: Man, you're heavy.

MIKE: I'm built like a truck. You wanna drag me more? I kinda like it cause the doctor says I got something wrong with my hip and this feels good.

ABBY: What's wrong with your hip?

MIKE: One of my legs is a few millimeters longer than the other one.

ABBY: For real?

MIKE: So now my hip's out of whack, and I feel it in my back. Hey, that rhymes. *(He pulls out a little notebook and pencil.)*
My hip's outta whack
I feel it in my back

ABBY: Get up. You gotta drag me around now.

(ABBY *and* MIKE *trade places. He drags her around.*)

ABBY: Can't they just put something in one of your shoes to even out your legs?

MIKE: Like an odor-eater?

ABBY: Something like that.

MIKE: My hip's outta whack,
I feel it in my back,
Trains run on a track,
Hmm… *(He stops dragging her.)* Can I ask you something?

ABBY: I don't know. Can you?

MIKE: Yeah. What's been your favorite kill?

ABBY: I got to shoot my old high school calculus teacher. I went in there and I was like, bet you're sorry you gave me a D now, asshole.

MIKE: I got to shoot this guy named Robbie who picked on me in fifth grade. He was a lot bigger back then, but I got some height on him since then. And I got a gun, so that helped.

ABBY: This job has its perks.

MIKE: How 'bout ice cream after you're done here?

ABBY: I'm real busy.

MIKE: You don't like ice cream?

ABBY: I'm not in an ice cream mood, Mike, okay?

MIKE: Yeah, okay.

ABBY: Alright?

MIKE: Yeah, no, it's fine.

ABBY: Some other time.

MIKE: What about coffee?

ABBY: Makes me jittery.

MIKE: Yeah, yeah, caffeine does that. Sure. Sure. Decaf, though?

ABBY: Really, Mike, after I'm through here I need to go home, take a nap before getting back to work tonight.

MIKE: Sure. No, I understand.

ABBY: Go home, Mike.

MIKE: Yeah, I should, I guess. I should cause I gotta pick up some dry cleaning. Well. You have a good day, Abby. *(He begins to exit, but stops and starts crying.)*

ABBY: Are you crying?

MIKE: *(Crying)* No.

ABBY: What's wrong?

MIKE: Harriett is gone.

ABBY: Where'd she go?

MIKE: There was a hole in my pocket. She fell out.

ABBY: You'll find another lucky bullet.

MIKE: There's only one lucky bullet. You fish it out of the chest of your first kill. You only have one of those.

ABBY: It's just a bullet.

MIKE: She dropped outta my pocket and I knew I lost something important. It's these dumb superstitious things that mean more than they actually mean. I guess…guess I've been feelin a bit maudlin. Job gets lonely for me sometimes. No matter how many nice people I meet, I always end up shooting them.

ABBY: Look, Mike, I gotta finish up with Johnny Duke.

MIKE: Yeah, I guess you're busy. Okay, well. See ya around, Abby.

(ABBY takes a bullet out of her pocket.)

ABBY: Hey.

(ABBY *gives* MIKE *the bullet.*)

MIKE: I can't take your lucky bullet.

ABBY: *(Goes back to* JOHNNY*)* What, I didn't hear you.

MIKE: I can't take—

ABBY: —Look, Mike, I'm working. Get outta here.

MIKE: Can I give you a hug?

ABBY: No.

MIKE: Who got this one?

ABBY: What?

MIKE: Who's chest you get this outta? Who's the first guy you shot?

(Pause)

ABBY: This guy I knew. While ago. Watched the movie Casablanca all the damn time. You ever see that one?

MIKE: Great movie.

ABBY: It's all right for an old movie.

MIKE: You wanna know my favorite movie?

ABBY: No.

MIKE: Toy Story. Bye, Abby. *(He exits.)*

Scene Six

(ABBY *enters* GWEN*'s apartment.* GWEN *is cleaning up a game of Monopoly)*

ABBY: Monopoly.

GWEN: Abby! You always sneak in like that. I'm—uh. Well, I'm just cleaning up here.

ABBY: Do you play Monopoly a lot?

GWEN: Oh. Um. Well, you know. Sometimes.

ABBY: By yourself?

GWEN: I like to practice. And, you know, Tess likes the little game pieces.

ABBY: She likes the game pieces.

GWEN: Yeah.

ABBY: Which one specifically.

GWEN: What? Oh, um, she likes, uh, she likes this horse thing.

ABBY: People in third world countries don't live as long as it takes to play this game. Hold up, Gwen, don't put that away yet.

GWEN: What?

ABBY: The piece that you got on your hand. Let me guess. The thimble.

GWEN: Yeah?

ABBY: Isn't it amazing that I knew that?

GWEN: Um. I'm just going to finish cleaning up, okay?

ABBY: So what was Wyatt doing here?

GWEN: We just played Monopoly.

ABBY: I can see that. Wyatt's got this weird thing with Monopoly. And you're certainly single now.

GWEN: You didn't think—? No. No no no, That's the last thing—Abby, I'm a widow.

ABBY: A do-it-yourself widow.

GWEN: We didn't do anything other than play Monopoly.

ABBY: Bullshit. You were married to Baxter, and he's about as pleasing as patio furniture.

GWEN: Baxter wasn't that bad.

ABBY: Wasn't that bad? You killed him.

GWEN: I know, but—

ABBY: Gwen, stay away from Wyatt, okay? He's going to try to make moves, and you can't let him do that to you. I don't know if you're attracted to his type, I'm sorry if you are, but he's a fucking prick. Promise me you'll stay away from him.

GWEN: Okay.

ABBY: You promise?

GWEN: Yeah, I promise.

ABBY: I'm trying to look out for you.

GWEN: I know you are.

ABBY: Glad we had that talk. You oughta finish cleaning that shit up, I hate Monopoly.

(LUCY *enters with her black bag.*)

LUCY: Hello, hello, hello.

ABBY: Gwen, we're gonna try something new today. Drugs.

GWEN: Oh, I don't do drugs.

ABBY: Drugs for killing.

LUCY: Abby, thank you for the invitation.

ABBY: Lucy, just do this quick so me and Gwen can go out and practice.

LUCY: I'll teach her as quickly as I can without sacrificing quality. Where's my test subject?

ABBY: Your what?

LUCY: Well, Abby, I was expecting you to supply a test subject for today's lesson.

ABBY: What do you need?

LUCY: A body.

ABBY: I think Miles had a hit this morning.

LUCY: Oh, no, Abby, veins must rise. I need a warm body with a beating heart.

ABBY: Well, I didn't know you needed a test subject. Can you wait while I go hunt down someone?

LUCY: I'm ready to do this right now.

ABBY: You didn't tell me you needed someone to work on.

LUCY: That's all right. We can work on you.

ABBY: Excuse me?

LUCY: My lesson plan is a three-part process. Part one focuses on the proper mechanics of sedation and termination. Part two is pharmaceuticals. Part three is the synthesis of mechanics and pharmaceuticals. Since this is only part one, mechanics, I'll be using saline—perfectly safe.

ABBY: What are mechanics?

LUCY: Needle insertion.

GWEN: Am I going to get to stick Abby with needles?

ABBY: Oh, fuck no.

GWEN: Come on, Abby, it'll be fun.

ABBY: Yeah, fun for you.

LUCY: Abby, this is a three part process. If I don't do this now, Gwen won't be ready to kill with this stuff for at least a week.

ABBY: A week? Why does it have to take that long?

LUCY: It's a delicate process. Do you want Gwen to learn this correctly or not?

(ABBY sits.)

LUCY: Science is grateful for your contribution. I'm going to need you to remove your coat.

(ABBY stands, takes off her coat.)

LUCY: Arms on the armrests please.

ABBY: Do you use band aids?

LUCY: I generally don't put band aids on dead men.

ABBY: I meant for me.

GWEN: I have band aids. They're actually Snoopy band aids, I hope you don't mind, Abby.

ABBY: Great.

(GWEN exits. LUCY restrains ABBY's arms to the chair.)

ABBY: Is this really necessary?

LUCY: For your safety.

ABBY: I'm not gonna go anywhere.

LUCY: This is how the job gets done.

ABBY: Are these really sharp needles?

LUCY: Sharp and sterile. Do you want me to wipe that sweat off your forehead before it gets in your eyes?

(GWEN enters.)

GWEN: Oooh, Abby, you look like you're gonna throw up.

ABBY: Oh, I'm fine, Gwen. I am fan-fucking-tastic.

GWEN: Do you want some music?

ABBY: No.

LUCY: Okay, Gwen, are you ready?

GWEN: I think so.

LUCY: Is there something wrong, Abby?

ABBY: Just stick me with the needle and get it over with.

LUCY: Ooooh, Abby, we're going to have to stick you with the needle more than once.

ABBY: What?

LUCY: Well, I have to demonstrate once, and then Gwen will follow my example, but it's rare to get it the first time. Even I didn't get it my first time.

ABBY: How long did it take you to get it?

LUCY: Nineteen tries, success on twenty. Okay, the first thing you need to do is locate an adequate vein in the arm. You can, of course, use any accessible vein on the body, but it takes practice and study to know those. We're going to start easy, all right? If the subject is cooperative, you can ask for them to rapidly open and close their hand in order to get the blood flowing and the veins popping. ...Like I said, if the subject is cooperative, you can ask them to rapidly open and close—

(ABBY *begins opening and closing her hand.*)

LUCY: —thank you. Gwen, are you ready?

GWEN: I'm ready.

LUCY: Okay, Abby, are you ready?

GWEN: Are you afraid of needles, Abby?

ABBY: *(Nervous laugh)* Of course not.

GWEN: Lucy, maybe we shouldn't do this if Abby's afraid of needles.

ABBY: I am *not* afraid of needles.

(LUCY *hands a needs a needle to* GWEN *and takes up one herself*)

LUCY: The standard technique is to hold the syringe between middle and index fingers, like this. Very good. Depending on the circumstance and the angle of injection you need to achieve, you may have to hold the syringe like this: *(Holds it in a* Psycho *shower scene stabbing grip)* See?

(GWEN *twirls the syringe expertly into this new position.*)

LUCY: Yes—very—very smooth, Gwen. Now we'll get into the advanced tutorial later, but, unfortunately, there are some instances where you will have to stab the victim.

ABBY: Can I have some music, anything, I don't care.

(GWEN *exits.*)

GWEN: *(Offstage)* Hmm. All I can find is Tess's music.

(GWEN *turns on some children's music, maybe something from a Disney movie. She reenters.*)

LUCY: Fear will only make your veins rupture.

(LUCY *squirts a fountain of saline into the air, taps out air bubbles.* GWEN *does the same*)

GWEN: Abby, I understand how you feel. Tess was terribly afraid of booster shots, but you know what you need to do? You just hold your breath. Close your eyes. And think about Disney World.

ABBY: I don't want to think about Disney World.

GWEN: Think about riding the tea cups at Disney World.

ABBY: I don't wanna think about—fuckin— *You* think about tea cups.

GWEN: Abby? Look at me. Hi. This will all be over very quickly, I promise. Okay? Now go like this: *(Holds her breath)*

(ABBY *holds her breath.*)

GWEN: Close your eyes.

(ABBY *closes her eyes.*)

GWEN: Tea cups.

LUCY: Are we all ready?

GWEN: I don't really feel right about this.

LUCY: Why not?

GWEN: I mean—look at her. Such misery.

LUCY: You need to practice, Gwen.

GWEN: I can just practice on myself. *(She begins tapping at the vein in her own arm.)*

LUCY: Um—what?

GWEN: You said I need practice.

LUCY: Well—yes—but not on *yourself.* It's quite complicated.

GWEN: You just kinda stab, right?

LUCY: Gwen dear—Gwen Gwen Gwen—oh, my little Gwen, there is so much you must learn. There is more *technique* than just "kinda stabbing". There is a surgical finesse that is acquired with years and years—

*(*GWEN *sticks the needle into her own arm—perfectly.* LUCY's *jaw drops.)*

ABBY: Is it over?

*(*ABBY *looks at* GWEN's *arm.)*

ABBY: Ohmygod. *(She passes out.)*

GWEN: Just like that, right? Lucy?

LUCY: Wow.

GWEN: I could totally do it on my other arm for more practice because I'm ambidextrous. Not many people know that.

LUCY: That was. Wow.

GWEN: See, Abby, I was thinking about Disney World and I hardly felt—Abby? Is she going to be okay?

LUCY: She was very impressed.

GWEN: She doesn't look very impressed. She looks very unconscious.

LUCY: Abby will be just fine. Here give me your arm.

(Lucy band aids Gwen's arm)

Gwen: Lucy.

Lucy: Yes?

Gwen: There's something I need to tell you.

Lucy: Is something wrong?

Gwen: Oh, um. You know Wyatt?

Lucy: What about Wyatt?

Gwen: I sort of killed him. Is that bad?

(Blackout)

END OF ACT ONE

ACT TWO

Scene One

(ABBY sits in her chair, still restrained, waking. She has a silly mustache drawn on her face. GWEN is in the room, behind ABBY. ABBY tries to get out of the restraints but can't.)

ABBY: Aw*fuck*me. *(Notices GWEN)* You gonna watch me flop around like a lunatic. *(Shifting the chair)* —Aagh. *(Contorts in the chair)*

GWEN: What are you doing?

ABBY: My underwear is going up my ass crack. Where is Lucy?

GWEN: Promise you won't get mad? If I undo the restraints will you promise you won't get mad?

ABBY: About what?

GWEN: Oh! Can I ask you a question? Quick question.

ABBY: What?

GWEN: It's no big deal. It's just something I want to know as long as you're restrained.

ABBY: What?

GWEN: Were you having an affair with my husband?

ABBY: *(Beat, avoiding the question)* Was I what with who?

GWEN: Were you having an affair with my husband Baxter? I was just curious…as to what you were doing here with Baxter the morning I shot him.

(*Pause*)

ABBY: Okay, look. I didn't know he had a daughter. And I knew he was married, vaguely. If it makes you feel any better, I didn't enjoy it. It was like wrestling a sweaty Rottweiler. If I screwed up your life, sorry. I didn't mean to hurt anybody.

GWEN: Abby, for somebody who doesn't want to hurt anybody, you chose a curious occupation.

ABBY: At some point you make a choice and stick with it, Gwen. Even after it shits in your mouth, y'know, whatever, you make it work.

GWEN: You could do something else. Something that doesn't make you angry all the time?

ABBY: (*Angry*) I'm not angry!

GWEN: Don't you want to do something other than kill people?

ABBY: This job is just what I am. It's all I know how to do.

(LUCY *enters.*)

LUCY: Excuse us a moment, Abby.

ABBY: Where were you?

LUCY: Out and about, excuse us please.

ABBY: Oh, neglect me. I'm unimportant. I don't mind being restrained to a chair, either. I don't care. Fuck you. I'm comfortable.

(GWEN *and* LUCY *aside*)

GWEN: Well?

LUCY: I got Wyatt down the fire escape, I think, well, his body took a— *(Indicates "tumble")* —down, down, down, and if he were alive, he would need a chiropractor. So he's down, *but* I am going to need some help lifting him to the car. Gwen, why does Abby have a mustache? It's very cute, but why?

GWEN: I was trying to keep Tess occupied with her coloring while you were moving you-know-what and I went to get some paper and in the time I was gone, literally two seconds, Tess had taken the marker to Abby's face. I haven't told Abby about the… *(Indicates mustache)*

(LUCY gets a make-up compact out of her purse and shows ABBY her reflection in the little mirror.)

LUCY: There comes a time in every girl's life when her body begins to change…

GWEN: I was going to tell you. That you have marker on your face. Tess had a little fun with her markers. On your face.

ABBY: That little shit.

GWEN: We'll undo your restraints, but you need to be good. Okay?

(GWEN and LUCY will undo ABBY's restraints.)

GWEN: This is all very funny when you stop to think about it, or at the very least, it may be funny in retrospect.

ABBY: Ohhh yeah yep.

GWEN: Tess likes you.

ABBY: She shouldn't like me.

LUCY: Why not?

ABBY: Cause I don't like kids. I don't trust them. They got agendas.

LUCY: *(Indicating the Monopoly guy on the box)* All you need is a top hat and you would look a little bit like this guy.

GWEN: I'm going to try to get an apology out of Tess, all right?

ABBY: I don't need an apology, Gwen. I don't need the little rat to say *I'm sorry* because, A) she won't mean it, and B) Don't teach her to be sorry for every little thing she does or she'll turn into you.

GWEN: What's wrong with that?

ABBY: Only everything.

GWEN: Why don't you like me?

ABBY: Not everybody is gonna like you. This isn't a popularity contest.

GWEN: You don't have to like me. I like me. You don't have to like me. I just want to know why you're so nasty to me. I want to know what, specifically, you don't like about me.

ABBY: You're difficult. You're a pain in the ass. I'm here to teach you how to kill and you're fighting me.

GWEN: I just don't want to. I'm not a violent person.

(COOPER enters, hopping into the room. His mouth and wrists are secured with duct tape, ankles bound. He eventually falls down and stays put. Pause)

ABBY: Who the fuck is that?

GWEN: Okay. This is my next door neighbor. We share a wall.

ABBY: Uh huh…

(ABBY tears the tape off COOPER's mouth)

COOPER: OW! Hi.

ABBY: Who are you?

COOPER: Cooper.

ABBY: Cooper?

COOPER: You got a mustache.

ABBY: What are you doing here?

COOPER: Oh. Huhn. See. I woke up in Gwen's bathtub.
You know? I haven't slept in three days. That's
the truth. Medical school is wrecking my circadian
rhythms. You ever use No Doz? You can see through
time. So I wake up in her bathtub and here I am
thinking it's a dream. Because the safest place during
a tornado is the bathtub. I thought I was having that
dream about the tornado and I was in the bathtub so
I wouldn't die. Cause I heard a gunshot before, came
over to see if Gwen was all right, and got knocked out.
(To LUCY*)* I've dreamed about you.

LUCY: Really?

GWEN: You two know each other?

LUCY: Well…

ABBY: What is he *doing here?*

GWEN: I was going to tell you about Cooper, but it was,
like, the secondary crisis. I can only handle one crisis at
a time. I may have screwed up. A little. Teeny tiny bit.

ABBY: Gee. Ya think?

*(*LUCY *helps* COOPER *out of his restraints.)*

GWEN: Um. Well. This is the part of our conversation
where you need to remain calm and not get angry and
this is especially the part where you don't yell at me
because it makes me very uncomfortable. Okay?

ABBY: Okay.

GWEN: Really?

ABBY: Sure.

GWEN: I shot Wyatt. He's dead. He made me play a game of Monopoly for my life. *Nobody should have to do that.*

ABBY: Wyatt is dead?

GWEN: You, uh… Hold on.

(GWEN *gets a tissue and wipes the mustache off* ABBY's *face.*)

Here. Hold still. I'm sorry, Abby.

ABBY: If you say you're sorry one more time I'm gonna belt you, okay? I woulda paid to see the look on Wyatt's face when you pulled the gun on him.

GWEN: He kinda looked like this: (*Makes a surprised face*)

ABBY: You gotta get rid of him. (COOPER)

GWEN: Get *rid* of him?

ABBY: You won't do it, then I'll do it. I'll show you how.

(COOPER *and* LUCY *kiss.*)

ABBY: No, no, no, no, no, no, no! Knock it off!

LUCY: What?

ABBY: Stop doing that.

LUCY: Abby. Cooper and I…

ABBY: You better not say it.

LUCY: We're in—

ABBY: Don't say it.

LUCY: Abby, we're in love.

ABBY: How nice. Well, fuck you and you too. Thank you all for making my job sunshine up the ass.

COOPER: Lucy and I got a thing goin. We're both night owls, and we got windows cross the street facing each

other. When she sits on her window ledge, she hugs
her knee like it's the most important part of her body.
It drives me wild.

LUCY: I know.

COOPER: You have the most beautiful silhouette I ever
seen.

LUCY: I notice how you chew on your pinky nail when
you're really concentrating.

COOPER: I noticed when you sat on that little cactus in
your windowsill.

LUCY: You noticed that?

COOPER: Yeah.

(ABBY *aims gun at* COOPER.)

COOPER: Whoa!

LUCY: Abby, put it down.

ABBY: Do you think I like cleaning up your messes,
covering for you. Do you think I wake up saying, gee, I
wonder how I can make Lucy hate me today.

LUCY: Okay, Abby, you have made your point. But
Cooper doesn't have any business with Ramone, he's
just a guy across the street.

COOPER: I'm just a guy.

LUCY: He came over to protect Gwen, an act of
kindness.

COOPER: I'm a nice guy.

LUCY: And he is now just in the wrong place at the
wrong time.

COOPER: My timing sucks.

LUCY: Now, Abby, I think you need to prioritize
your anger before you mismanage your emotional
resources, yes?

ABBY: What?

LUCY: Please don't point your boom stick at us.

(ABBY *lowers the gun.*)

ABBY: Lucy, you fall in love every ten minutes; you're like a one-woman flock of horny rabbits; it's *inaffective*. It gets in the way of your work. Do you see me falling in love with every dumbass who crosses the line with Ramone? Do you see me getting misty eyed for every blood splattered Romeo. When love comes screaming through the window, sometimes you just have to ignore it.

(*Lights up on* MIKE, *standing outside the apartment looking up*)

MIKE: ABBY! I LOVE YOU!

(*They all go to the window.*)

MIKE: I found Harriett! She was stuck in the lining of my coat! Abby, catch!

(MIKE *tosses a bullet to the window.* ABBY *catches it*)

ABBY: Mike, this isn't my bullet! This is Harriett!

MIKE: I know! I got yours! If you want it back, you have to go on a date with me!

ABBY: *What*?

MIKE: I want ice cream and I don't want ice cream with anyone other than you!

ABBY: Mike!

MIKE: I can't hear you, Abby, my heart's pounding in my head and the only thing it'll let in is a "yes".

ABBY: (*After a pause*) Yes.

MIKE: Yes?!

ABBY: If I have to repeat myself I'll beat the shit out of you!

MIKE: I have to go shoot a guy now…but I'll be thinking of you!

(*Lights down on* MIKE)

LUCY: You're blushing.

ABBY: No I'm not.

LUCY: That's really cute, Abby.

GWEN: (*Tunefully*) Abby's got a boyfriend.

ABBY: Shut up.

GWEN: That's the sweetest thing I have ever seen. A declaration of love from the street to the window.

COOPER: Seems like a cool guy. Kinda reminds me of this one guy in my skeletal structure class…

ABBY: (*Overlap above*) Get outta here.

COOPER: What?

ABBY: Go away.

COOPER: Lucy, I gotta ask you cause if I don't do it now, I'm not sure I got courage enough to do it ever. You wanna go out for real sometime?

LUCY: For real?

COOPER: No more of this stuff in the windows.

LUCY: You want to go on a date with me?

COOPER: Oh, yeah, more than anything.

LUCY: A date. A real date. It's been a while since I've been on a date where I haven't had to kill my date after the goodnight kiss.

COOPER: I'm pretty looped on No Doz and Red Bull right now, so, yeah, I'm okay with just about anything that could possibly happen.

LUCY: Do you want to make this night last a little longer.

COOPER: And then tomorrow, we can do ice cream and we can double date with Abby and that Mike guy.

ABBY: Hey, Lucy, why don't you take Cooper for a walk?

COOPER: I'm not a dog. I don't just take orders.

LUCY: Cooper, let's go.

COOPER: Okay.

(COOPER *and* LUCY *exit.* ABBY *goes to the phone, dials.*)

GWEN: What are you going to wear on your first date? You would look great in red.

ABBY: I only said yes because I want my lucky bullet back.

GWEN: Then why did you give him your bullet?

ABBY: I'm not going out with him. I'll tell him I'm sick.

GWEN: You'll break his heart.

ABBY: You should know that a relationship with a hitman is no picnic. You *shot* Baxter.

GWEN: There was nothing good about Baxter. Murder isn't a good substitute for divorce, but, honestly Abby, Baxter's most positive quality was that he cleaned the dryer's lint screen. And he didn't even do the laundry. He was obsessive compulsive about picking the lint off the screen.

ABBY: *(On phone)* Ramone. It's Abby. We gotta talk, Bar West in a half hour, I'm not talking on the phone… half hour. Yeah, bye. *(Hangs up)* You shouldn't stay here tonight.

GWEN: Why not?

ABBY: You'll need to pack up some shit, take your daughter, go somewhere else tonight.

GWEN: Where should we go?

ABBY: It's for the best if I don't know where you are. You understand?

GWEN: You wouldn't, though? …Would you?

(ABBY *picks up the teddy bear, looks at it, sets it down. Picks up a packet of papers, flips through it.*)

GWEN: That's something Tess and I worked on together a few weeks ago when she said she wanted to write lots and lots of books.

ABBY: *Princess Tess and the Moon Monsters.*

GWEN: It's her idea, her story, I just wrote it down. She drew the pictures. Worked really hard on it. Do you want to read it?

ABBY: I gotta go.

GWEN: Take it with you, you can return it when you finish reading it, okay? Maybe things will work out fine and we won't have to hurt each other. Right?

ABBY: I don't think it's going to end that way, Gwen. I've written a few stories myself. My stories always end badly.

GWEN: Then you'll do what you need to do. And I'll do what I need to do.

ABBY: Then we'll both do what we need to do.

GWEN: That's right.

ABBY: Glad to know you're learning something.

GWEN: Goodnight, Abby.

ABBY: Goodnight, Gwen. (*She exits.*)

Scene Two

(A bar. RAMONE *sits and drinks.* ABBY *enters. She doesn't sit next to him. They seem to be unaware of each other. Some time passes)*

RAMONE: Are you angry?

ABBY: It wasn't a part of our agreement.

RAMONE: I know.

ABBY: I'm only a little offended you sent Wyatt to kill Gwen. I told you I would do something. You obviously didn't think I could.

RAMONE: I'm sorry you were offended. Abbs, you were a different woman before I got a hold of you. Now I'm sorry it came down to me taking action here, terminating your pet project. I know you're angry about a lot. Wyatt still needs your car. Gwen is dead. I don't expect you to like me, but I'm the boss, and I need you to—at the very least—respect that.

ABBY: You've never had a hold on me.

RAMONE: I did for at least one kill. *(Pause)* Your first kill changes you. My first kill changed me.

ABBY: I took the job, it was my decision.

RAMONE: Immediately after I hired you, I did my research. I had to find out about you. I had to find who you loved.

ABBY: Who I loved.

RAMONE: Yes.

ABBY: I didn't love him

RAMONE: He loved you.

ABBY: How do you know that? Did he say that?

RAMONE: Yeah, he did. He said that. We got to talking about the women in our lives, during our game of cards, and you were his Angel. He was trying to win a pretty penny on the straight flush he had, said he wanted to buy you just the right engagement ring. Something nice, but not too flashy because he knew you wouldn't like that.

ABBY: He was going to ask me to marry him?

RAMONE: You didn't know that? I thought you knew that.

ABBY: No.

RAMONE: His hand went to the Jack and mine went to the King. It was a pretty wild bet. High stakes. The pilot lost big. The flight attendant and the pilot. Must've been romantic for you two. Flings in Paris, flings in Rome, wherever you wanted to go.

ABBY: Wherever we wanted.

RAMONE: He told me you'd watch Casablanca with him even though he knew you didn't like it. Because no matter how many times you watched it, the ending wouldn't change. *(Pause)* That was your test Abby. If you could kill the man you loved, you could kill for me. I had to test you, Abby. I want you to understand that.

ABBY: I understand.

RAMONE: I had to make sure you could do any job I asked of you. It's my job to test people. That's why I sent Wyatt after Gwen. That was her test.

ABBY: That wasn't a test. It was an execution.

RAMONE: It was a test.

ABBY: It was an unfair test.

RAMONE: It was still a test that—honestly, if she could've passed it, she could have my job. Wyatt scares the bajeezus outta me the way he works.

ABBY: So who's getting the promotion?

RAMONE: Wyatt.

(Pause)

ABBY: What if I had a kid?

RAMONE: What?

ABBY: What if I had a kid?

RAMONE: Is there something you want to tell me?

ABBY: I'm curious. It's just a question.

RAMONE: Then it's not an issue.

ABBY: What if I made it an issue.

RAMONE: Are you going to make it an issue?

ABBY: I don't know.

RAMONE: Then it's not an issue.

ABBY: So you would prefer it not be an issue.

RAMONE: I can't even imagine it.

ABBY: Excuse me?

RAMONE: I've known you for a while now.

ABBY: I am a woman, aren't I?

RAMONE: Sorta.

ABBY: What the fuck you mean sorta?

RAMONE: I mean, you're you. The way I know you, I don't think of you as... Now, that isn't to say...

ABBY: Uh huh.

RAMONE: My point is, Abby, you don't strike me as the mothering type.

ABBY: How do you want me to strike you? Fist or open palm?

RAMONE: Look, Abby, Gwen couldn't cut it, if that's what you're angry about—

ABBY: Would you fire me?

RAMONE: For what?

ABBY: If I were a mother would you have even hired me to begin with?

RAMONE: I knew Gwen would be a bad influence on you. Abby, you do a good job as is. I don't tell you that enough.

ABBY: Okay, if I were Gwen and I passed your test and I was very, very good at my job and I had a child, would you fire me?

RAMONE: I don't live by hypotheticals. How about a drink? That's an actual, not a hypothetical.

ABBY: No.

RAMONE: Come on. I'm buying. What do you want?

ABBY: I gotta drive.

(RAMONE stares at ABBY.)

ABBY: What? Sorry if it disappoints you that I don't drink and drive.

RAMONE: Drive what?

ABBY: A car.

RAMONE: Whose car?

ABBY: My car.

(Pause)

RAMONE: You must be upset I'm not promoting you.

ABBY: You disappointed I'm not flying into hysterics?

RAMONE: Just surprised you're not more upset, that's all. And I want you to know that nobody can beat Wyatt. Not even you. That's not a slam on your skills. You're good, Abby, but you're not that good. That's just a fact as I see it. I really don't tell you enough how good a job you do. You're on an even keel with me,

Abbs. Wouldn't want you to do anything to blow it.
There's always someone else who can replace you.
Easily. *(Pause)* Is there anything you want to tell me? I
have the funniest sense you want to tell me something.

ABBY: I have nothing more to say to you.

RAMONE: Drive safely.

(ABBY exits.)

Scene Three

(ABBY enters LUCY's apartment)

ABBY: Lucy. Hey Lucy, wake up.

*(COOPER answers the door. He's wearing only boxers and is
brushing his teeth.)*

ABBY: Oh. You.

COOPER: Hey, Abby. What's up?

ABBY: Not much.

COOPER: Cool.

ABBY: How you doing?

COOPER: Awesome.

ABBY: Yeah, I bet.

(GWEN and LUCY enter.)

ABBY: I told you to go away.

GWEN: I didn't want to.

ABBY: *(Gives car keys to GWEN)* You need to go.

GWEN: Abby, I can't go. I need to take Tess to Career
Day in the morning.

ABBY: Oh, fuck Career Day, take my car and go.

GWEN: But…Tess is asleep.

ABBY: (*Overlap above, to offstage*) Hey, Tess, snot-monkey, wake up, you're going for a drive.

GWEN: Shhhh, she hasn't been sleeping well, I don't want to wake her.

ABBY: You have to go.

GWEN: I'm not going to be scared off. I'm not going to be intimidated. I have a life here and I'm not just going to take off.

ABBY: You're not gonna have much of a life if you stay.

(MIKE *and* RAMONE *enter.*)

RAMONE: (*To* COOPER) Who the hell are you?

COOPER: I'm Cooper. What's up?

RAMONE: Do I know you?

COOPER: Lot a people say I look like someone they know, like I got one of those faces, you know?

LUCY: Now would be a good time for you to go.

COOPER: But I'm not dressed.

LUCY: That's okay.

COOPER: But my shoes—

LUCY: Tomorrow.

(LUCY *pushes* COOPER *out of the apartment. He exits.*)

RAMONE: Well this is interesting. Are you ladies having a slumber party?

LUCY: Oh, yes! And we're microwaving S'mores later! Would you like a s'more, Ramone? I think you'd like a S'more.

RAMONE: It's nice to see you again, Gwen. How long has it been? Since the wedding?

GWEN: Yeah, I think so.

RAMONE: You look good. How's your daughter doing?

GWEN: She's fine.

RAMONE: Good to hear. Well. I wish we could be meeting under different circumstances. We should just get right down to it. It's late, everybody's tired, no need to waste any more time than we have to. Gwen, I'll just ask you straight up. Do you want this job?

GWEN: No.

RAMONE: You're probably not the right fit for this organization, am I right?

GWEN: I never wanted to be a part of Baxter's business.

RAMONE: Well, hey, I never thought you should be a part of this to begin with. Abby thought she could rope you into this life, and when Abby has her mind set on something, she's a bull dog to the very end. Bull dog with a big, sharp set of teeth. Ruthless. That's admirable. I'm lucky to have her around. (*Referring to* LUCY) This one, I'm not so sure about. We'll get to your evaluation later. I'm only so good at multi-tasking, you know? I have my limit. Our deal here was that Abby was going to train you to do this job. You don't want the job. There's an old saying, Gwen, and you all listen up too. You can lead a horse to water but you can't make him put a bullet in somebody's brain. If you don't want a job, nobody can force you to work. That's the simple truth. However, if you don't want this particular job, we're going to have to sever some ties tonight. Abby?

ABBY: What?

RAMONE: What do you mean "what?" Tell Gwen the deal.

ABBY: She knows the deal. I told her the deal straight up.

RAMONE: Maybe if you remind Gwen about the deal, she'll change her no to a yes.

ABBY: Gwen, you can't do this job, I'm going to kill you and your daughter.

GWEN: You won't do it, will you? You won't do it.

ABBY: Gwen, it's what I do. I kill things.

GWEN: This is different. You know me. You know Tess. We're friends.

RAMONE: She's killed more than friends before.

GWEN: Lucy. Help me.

RAMONE: Lucy, you wag that tongue of yours, consider yourself fired. Now I've been lenient on your new methods, but keep your mouth shut if you want to keep your job.

GWEN: Lucy?

LUCY: Oh. *Well*. No, I won't say anything more…

RAMONE: *What?*

LUCY: She killed Wyatt.

(*Pause*)

RAMONE: Funny that Abby didn't enlighten me sooner. Very very interesting. Well now. Abby. Why don't you go on and finish up Wyatt's job here, and we'll see what we can do about your promotion.

(ABBY *pulls her gun out and puts it to* GWEN*'s head. Pause*)

ABBY: Fuck! FUCK!

RAMONE: Something the matter, Abby?

ABBY: No. I'm fine!

RAMONE: Then can we get back to business here.

ABBY: Yeah! Hold on. Give me a second.

RAMONE: It's getting late.

ABBY: Give me one second. One second. Give me one second. (*Puts gun to* GWEN's *head. Pause. She lowers the gun.*)

RAMONE: Mike, you're going to have to finish Abby's job here.

(MIKE *nods. Puts his gun to* GWEN's *head.*)

MIKE: Um.

RAMONE: What?

(MIKE *lowers the gun.*)

MIKE: I like Abby. I like Abby a whole lot. I've liked her ever since I first set my eyes on her and she said, "What are you looking at, slackjaw?" We have an ice cream date. I don't want to muck this up by shooting one of her friends in the head. That's the quickest way to muck up a first date.

(RAMONE *looks at* ABBY *for confirmation.*)

ABBY: We're having ice cream.

RAMONE: This is ridiculous. You want a job done right, you have to do it yourself.

(RAMONE *is about to go for his gun, but* GWEN *puts her gun to* RAMONE's *head. Pause*)

RAMONE: Did Wyatt make you play Monopoly?

GWEN: Yes.

RAMONE: Did you beat him at Monopoly?

GWEN: Yes.

RAMONE: I told him, one of these days someone was going to beat him.

GWEN: He passed up all sorts of opportunities with the cheaper properties. He spent all his money on houses too early in the game. And I'm not even going to get into his botched strategy with the railroads.

RAMONE: You can't wait on the railroads. And then Boardwalk...

GWEN: Completely overrated.

RAMONE: Exactly.

GWEN: Exactly.

(GWEN lowers her gun. Pause)

RAMONE: *(To ABBY)* I'm gonna let you go.

ABBY: What?

RAMONE: I'm letting you go as a regular employee.

ABBY: You're firing me?

RAMONE: I'll keep you as a consultant. You're going to finish training your replacement here.

ABBY: What?

GWEN: Replacement?

RAMONE: And if there are some freelance opportunities—

ABBY: *Freelance.*

RAMONE: Yes. Freelance.

ABBY: You're *demoting* me?

RAMONE: I'm restructuring my human resources.

ABBY: This is un-fucking-believable. You have no professional tact, shit head. Why don't you just *fire* me!

RAMONE: Fine. You're fired.

ABBY: W—

RAMONE: Gwen, as of right now, you're on the payroll. If you shot Wyatt, you are one in a million, and I'm not going to pass up the opportunity to have you work for me.

GWEN: I don't want a job. I don't want this! I have a choice.

RAMONE: Of course you have a choice. Work or death. Everybody's gotta make a living.

GWEN: I won't do this.

RAMONE: Don't you even want to know how much money you'll be making with me?

GWEN: No! *(Beat)* How much?

(RAMONE takes out a pocket notebook, writes down a figure, shows GWEN.)

GWEN: Ohmygod. Really?

RAMONE: Really.

GWEN: I've never earned that much in my entire life. That's per year?

RAMONE: Per year? Ha, you're cute. It's per month.

(GWEN is stunned.)

RAMONE: Now I'm going to have to cover for Wyatt's scheduled hits, and he has a nine A M appointment. Why don't you join me for that one? We can chat, maybe have some breakfast after?

GWEN: Nine A M?

RAMONE: Is there a problem with nine?

GWEN: I have to go to Career Day.

RAMONE: Afraid not, Gwen.

GWEN: I have to go to Career Day!

RAMONE: Hey, guess what. I don't care. See you at nine.

GWEN: But.

RAMONE: Nine.

GWEN: I...I guess I have to tell Tess I can't go tomorrow.

RAMONE: Good.

(GWEN *exits.*)

RAMONE: See, Abby, when you want to get a "yes" out of somebody, don't start with ideology and principle. Start with a number and work backwards.

ABBY: How much are you paying her?

RAMONE: None a your business. Mike, you're on for that eight A M hit tomorrow.

MIKE: Sure am.

RAMONE: We'll talk the details on the way down.

MIKE: Goodnight.

RAMONE: Abby. Thanks for your hard work. I really appreciate it. I'll get you a watch.

(MIKE *and* RAMONE *exit. Pause)*

ABBY: I just got fired.

LUCY: He would've kept you as a consultant.

ABBY: Consultant is just another word for "demoted pile of dog shit."

LUCY: It was still a job. Now you have no job. The bright side is…you can do absolutely anything you want with your day tomorrow.

ABBY: I don't want to do anything.

LUCY: You can't sit home and pout.

ABBY: Yes I can. I can also drink and watch soaps.

LUCY: The Abby I know doesn't pout.

ABBY: Leave me alone.

(GWEN *enters.*)

GWEN: Abby?

ABBY: *What?*

GWEN: I need your help.

ABBY: Did you miss the part of the evening where I got fired and you replaced me?

GWEN: Oh, I was there for that.

ABBY: You don't need my help. You're good at killing. Congratulations.

GWEN: No, no, I don't need help with work. Um. Abby. I uh. I was talking to Tess and…are you going to be all right, Abby?

ABBY: I'm fine.

GWEN: Well. I was talking to Tess. I, see, I sort of made her a promise.

ABBY: What did you promise her?

Scene Four

(ABBY *in the car, currently parked.* TESS *is in the backseat.*)

ABBY: *(To Tess)* You're short, you know that? You're like a midget. I was watching this T V show about some circus, and they fired midgets out of cannons into swimming pools. So you get a job with the circus, you get a crash helmet with your name on it. And you can play with the monkeys that pee and shit all over the place, so there's a bright side to everything.

(MIKE *enters the car.*)

MIKE: Thanks for inviting me to Career Day.

ABBY: Tess, this is Mike Sanders. Mike, Tess.

MIKE: Hi, Tess. …She's like a little person.

ABBY: *(Looks in rearview mirror)* Put on your seat belt.

MIKE: Can we still make a stop before we get to the school?

ABBY: Yeah.

MIKE: Great. I was just thinking how much I loved career day when I was a kid. This one kid's dad invented the magnetic paper clip holder. It was amazing. ...Feels like we're married and we have a kid and everything. You want kids?

ABBY: With you?

MIKE: Okay.

ABBY: We'd have idiot children.

MIKE: Then in general?

ABBY: I'd fuck it up.

MIKE: Kids are like Slinkies. I mean, you can't throw them down the stairs, but they spring back from a lot of stuff.

ABBY: I bet a kid like Tess is a big pain in the ass. We'd argue about what states could beat up other states, and she'd pick Maine and justify it in lobsters. *(To Tess in back)* Hey. I said put on your seat belt. I hit a telephone pole, you're gonna fly through the windshield and liquefy on the pavement. I don't wanna explain to your mom why I had to bring you home in your thermos.

MIKE: You think about having kids?

ABBY: No.

MIKE: Never?

ABBY: Sometimes.

MIKE: Me too. Sometimes.

ABBY: Not a lot.

MIKE: No, not a lot. *(Beat)* Let me know if you want to.

ABBY: What?

MIKE: Have kids.

ABBY: I think we should have ice cream first.

MIKE: Sounds good.

ABBY: All right, Mike, you better make this quick.

MIKE: Be right back. *(He exits.)*

ABBY: *(Lights a cigarette, smokes)* You smoke? Want to? Your mom is going to tell you that smoking isn't cool, but look at this. *(Smokes cool)* I forget what that's called, but its sophisticated. You whip that out at parties and people are like, yeah, she's cool. ...Oh, stop coughing you big faker. Hey, enough already, you're not dying. All right, all right. *(She puts out her cigarette.)* I'm not telling you to start because, between you and me, I'm starting to cough up some strange shit.

(MIKE enters, sprayed with blood.)

ABBY: Okay, you're gonna have to stay in the car for Career Day.

MIKE: Why?

ABBY: Did you bring a change of clothes?

MIKE: This is good because it looks like I came right from work *to* Career Day.

ABBY: Ohh, man…

MIKE: What?

ABBY: Well—Mike—this means I have to go in there by myself!

MIKE: Aren't you gonna bring Tess in?

ABBY: Yeah—but I wanted you in there with me because people seem to like you, and if you were there, maybe I wouldn't have to talk.

MIKE: I'm sorry I hit a major artery at close range.

ABBY: No, no, that's okay. I'm—nervous.

MIKE: I once took a public speaking class, and they always said that if you're nervous about giving a speech then you should imagine your audience naked.

ABBY: Mike, this is a Kindergarten class.

MIKE: Wow, then that's really inappropriate advice. How about: take some time right now to think about what you're going to talk about.

ABBY: I can talk about how life is an endless vortex of disappointment.

MIKE: How old are these kids?

ABBY: Five? *(Looks back at Tess for confirmation)* Five.

MIKE: Maybe you can talk about something else.

ABBY: Look, I don't know what I'm going to talk about. I got fired. I'm going to Career Day without a career. I got nothing to share with a class fulla kids.

MIKE: Nothing wrong with making stuff up. The school should be up here on the right. See, you can say whatever you want to say because you're not defined by this one thing that you probably couldn't talk about anyway for legal reason.

ABBY: You think they'll let me smoke during Career Day?

MIKE: Probably not. I got gum if you want that.

ABBY: Yeah.

(MIKE gets gum, gives it to ABBY, she chews it.)

MIKE: I really can't go in? I was gonna say I was an astronaut. Want your lucky bullet back?

ABBY: I got yours.

MIKE: Harriet is a great bullet. She's gotten me through some tough times. Can I ask you something?

ABBY: I don't know. Can you?

MIKE: Yeah. What's your bullet's name?

ABBY: Nothing.

MIKE: That's a silly name for a lucky bullet.

ABBY: My bullet's name is—don't make a big deal out of it, okay?

MIKE: Okay.

ABBY: Ozzie.

MIKE: Ozzie and Harriet.

ABBY: Yeah.

MIKE: I like it.

ABBY: We're here. *(Beat)* You'll wait here? You won't drive off and leave me stranded?

MIKE: I'll be here when you come out.

ABBY: *(To the back seat)* You ready?

MIKE: Will you be all right in there?

ABBY: Yeah, sure.

MIKE: You'll do great.

ABBY: How hard could this be, right? It's just a bunch of stupid kids.

Scene Five

(Career Day)

ABBY: Hi. My name is Abby. It's good to be here at Career Day. All your parents' jobs have sounded…fun. Especially Jonathan's dad who described working for twenty years at the same bank. You know the only job worse than that? My uncle used to masturbate turkeys for a living.

Okay. Look. I'm not Tess's mom. Tess's mom now does my job. Or the job that I used to do. Yeah. Today was my first day off in a while. So I got up. Took a shower. Got dressed. I made toast. I burned it.

This place smells like school. I hated school. Well I liked this one science class in high school. Our teacher,

Mister Gerard, wanted to prove that a body can only
digest so much lactose—how many of you like lactose?
Okay, nobody. How many of you like milk? Milk and
lactose are the same thing. That was a trick question.
Mister Gerard, well he had all of us bring in a gallon
of whole milk and a bucket, and we drank and drank
until we threw up. In our buckets. You can try that
at home. Mister Gerard was a great teacher. He got
fired for that class. But I learned a lot about the human
digestive system that day.
Here's my official Career Day advice. You're all going
to grow up and get jobs, right? Some of you will hate
your jobs, some of you won't really care, the lucky ones
will like their jobs. You may get fired. No matter how
good of a job you do, you might get fired for bullshit
reasons…what, I can't say "shit"? Why the fuck not?
…I can't say that either? All right. Shit. Sorry. I don't
know. I been sitting here with all of you listening to
all your parents with all their careers and I thought
maybe coming in here today would give me some
ideas, but it hasn't. Maybe you got some ideas. If you
got some ideas, then that's good and this wasn't a big
waste of time. (Takes out Tess's fairy tale) I'm jumping
to show and tell now. I got this fairy tale. Tess wrote it
and her mom helped her with it. Tess did the pictures.
Anyway, I like it. I don't know why. Some reason. The
pictures are weird, but Tess is a weird kid. I'll just read
some of this and call it a day, if that's okay. It's called
Princess Tess and the Moon Monsters.
"Once upon a time, there was a princess. She liked to
run and jump rope and go to the pool in the summer.
But more than anything, she liked to watch the moon
change. Full to half to a teeny tiny sliver. But one
night, it stopped changing. So the princess climbed on
her rocket-ship, and blasted off to the moon because
someone had to do something. And the princess could

do anything. Anything at all. She could even fix the
moon."

END OF PLAY

www.ingramcontent.com/pod-product-compliance
Lightning Source LLC
Chambersburg PA
CBHW070023110426
42741CB00034B/2416